For

## *Secrets of Happiness and Success*

### Roger Richie

**Funeral Home Owner (Retired 2019)
Licensed Funeral Director and Embalmer
Missouri (Since 1971) and Illinois (Since 1985)**

Copyright©2020, Roger Richie
All rights reserved.

Look For Good, LLC
rprichie48@gmail.com

ISBN: 978-1-7353234-0-3

Design by Roger Richie
United States

*Look for Good* and it always appears.

"When I *look for good* in people and in life, more of it always appears."

Roger Richie

*Look for Good* and it always appears.

This book is dedicated to
Linda Henry, my wife, life partner
and the light of my life.

*Look for Good* and it always appears.

# Contents

## MY LIFE AWAKENS

| | |
|---|---|
| Why I Wrote This Book | 1 |
| What Do I Want? | 3 |
| What I Believe in a "Nutshell" | 5 |

## <u>MY LIFE IS ABUNDANT</u>
### (Compiled since 1981)

| | | |
|---|---|---|
| 1. | Look for THINKING | 8 |
| 2. | Look for LOVE | 11 |
| 3. | Look for KINDNESS | 13 |
| 4. | Look for GRATITUDE | 15 |
| 5. | Look for PEACE | 17 |
| 6. | Look for WELL-BEING | 19 |
| 7. | Look for PROSPERITY & SUCCESS | 20 |
| 8. | Look for FORGIVENESS | 22 |
| 9. | Look for COMPASSION | 23 |
| 10. | Look for HAPPINESS | 25 |
| 11. | Look for ATTITUDE | 27 |
| 12. | Look for TODAY | 29 |
| 13. | Look for COURAGE | 31 |
| 14. | Look for CHARACTER | 33 |
| 15. | Look for SERVICE | 35 |
| 16. | Look for JOY | 37 |
| 17. | Look for GOODNESS | 38 |
| 18. | Look for HOPE | 40 |
| 19. | Look for PURPOSE & GOALS | 42 |
| 20. | Look for PATIENCE | 44 |
| 21. | Look for HUMILITY | 45 |
| 22. | Look for SELF-CONTROL | 47 |
| 23. | Look for RESPONSIBILITY | 49 |
| 24. | Look for TRUST | 51 |
| 25. | Look for LAUGHTER | 52 |
| 26. | Look for MINDFULNESS | 53 |
| 27. | Look for HEALTH | 55 |

# Contents Continued

**AFFIRMATIONS**      57

**SIMPLE LIFE INSTRUCTIONS**      58

**ABOUT THE AUTHOR**      59

**BOOKMARK**      61

*Look for Good* and it always appears.

# **MY LIFE AWAKENS**

*Look for Good* and it always appears.

# WHY I WROTE THIS BOOK

I am extremely grateful for the many obstacles and setbacks in my life. Because of them I learned to *look for good.* When I choose to *look for good*, it always appears. With goodness, I have grown and learned many lessons to become the loving, kind, happy and successful person I am today. I am still a work in progress—learning every day.

Just when did the big obstacles and setbacks begin? When did my life awaken?

It was Friday, December 18, 1981, the week before Christmas. At age 33, I was laid off from the funeral home where I had been a funeral director and embalmer for more than 10 years. As a husband, father of three young daughters, owner of a modest new home and the only parent working outside the home, I was scared to death. Life changed dramatically. It was frightening, chaotic and at the same time, a great adventure, changing my life for the better.

Within several months I formed my own small corporation, bought the formulas and mixing equipment of an embalming chemical company that was closed and began an unpredictable journey. Soon I was manufacturing and selling chemicals as well as providing freelance embalming services at funeral homes within about a 50-mile radius of St. Louis, Missouri.

In 1984 I continued my professional growth by buying and remodeling a building to form an independent embalming service and crematory company. Due to a divorce in 1993, I sold my business to an employee. At that time, I had grown the business into the largest embalming/crematory company, working for funeral homes only (not the public), in the State of Missouri.

Also at that point I was unemployed, homeless, had a four-year old Ford Mustang and, thankfully, had no debt. I secured a position at a local St. Louis funeral home and advanced my position to owner/president in 2006 and sold that ownership in 2019 to step into retirement at age 71.

From 1981 to 2019, I had 38 years of situations – questions, problems, obstacles, difficulties, uncertainty, perplexity, debates, lessons, barricades, snags, and many wonderful joys and opportunities. I have grown a lot. I met my wife and sweetheart, Linda Henry, in 2008 and can now envision the rest of my life with a real partner and trusted advocate.

It's these 38 years that I am most grateful for in my life. They awakened me to the possibilities life has to offer. They inspired me to learn, grow and think for myself – to become the best person I could be. I am still working on that.

This book, *LOOK For GOOD – Secrets of Happiness and Success,* is part of the knowledge that I began acquiring in 1981 and is a compilation from numerous sources and my own experiences. I would like to share what I have learned with you. I hope this knowledge will bring you many wonderful joys, opportunities and support your own process of becoming the best person you can be.

The information I am about to share is not new. The ideas are concise and simple. Hopefully my book will resonate with you where others have not. Perhaps, as the saying goes, the student is ready and the teacher has appeared.

Without question, the very first <u>secret</u> of happiness and success is the following affirmation. Please write it down and carry it with you. Repeat it to yourself many times each day, as I do.

"I become what I *think* about. I attract what I *think* about."

*Look for Good* and it always appears.

# WHAT DO I WANT?

Most people don't get what they want in life because…. <u>they don't know what they want</u>! This is really important. Read that again. They don't know what they want! They wander through life like a rudderless sailboat going with the prevailing wind in any direction it takes them, casually wishing for things.

People must *think* to learn what they want to be, do and have! Thinking is the hardest work there is. That's why so few people do it and why they don't get what they want.

The thinking process works like this: Thinking creates thoughts; Thoughts create words; Words create beliefs; Beliefs create actions; Actions create habits; Habits create character; Character creates service; Service creates a *life*.

Along with the work of thinking, there is a price to pay to achieve what is wanted: time, talents, energy, education, money, delayed gratification, etc. It is work. What do I really want?

The clearer I am in my mind about what I want and what I am willing to do to get it, the greater the probability that I will achieve what I want. I think, speak and act only on what I want. I embrace and focus on what I want. Most people fail by focusing on what they don't want.

Think about what you want to be, do and have in each of many areas: health, relationships, finances, career, spiritual, retirement or recreation. What would happiness in each of these areas look like? Picture it. Visualize it. Focus on it. Write it down, reflect and think about it often. Be flexible, thoughts change.

If you don't know what happiness and success in any area would look like, think about it. What would make you truly happy in your relationships? Ask yourself questions. Who? What? Why? When? Where?

With no clear goal, you're like an archer with no target. How could you ever hit a bullseye? If you aim at nothing, you'll hit it every time.

I become what I think about.          I attract what I think about.

The story of my life is also like a movie. Only in my life movie, I am the producer, director, editor, writer, main character AND the hero. I create the story of my life, act out my part and live the story from start to finish. My movie, my life, is all based on my thinking. I can change the story and its ending on a daily basis, actually moment by moment, by changing my thinking. I'm in charge. It's my thoughts. It's my life.

Regardless of my current situation, I ask myself, "How does my life story proceed from here?" It's up to me. I have to think! What do I want and what am I waiting for? If not NOW, when? If not HERE, where? Remember and repeat: I become what I think about. I attract what I think about.

Remembering that at some point in life I'll be dead, investing myself in what I really want now becomes a lot easier. Things like embarrassment, fear, worry, anger, guilt, pride or ego seem to disappear. That leaves me with what's important and really matters: loving and serving others.

My suggestion is to read the book cover to cover. Then each day with your morning coffee, starting with Thinking #1, read a word and immerse yourself in the ideas and concepts of the attached statements. You might highlight the statements that standout to you. After 27 days, start over. During your daily reading, think, "What do I want to be, do and have?"

To find what you want, you must *look for good*. When you *look for good* in people and in life, more of it always appears. I want your life to awaken. I want your life to be abundant.

The ideas on the following pages will be a guide. I hope you enjoy the journey.

*Look for Good* and it always appears.

# What I Believe, In a "Nutshell"
**(Simple thoughts that put my life in order)**

I am the only one who thinks inside my head.

I am master of my thoughts and thoughts become things.

I can create, choose and change my thoughts.

I think, speak and act only on what I want.

I become what I think about.

I attract what I think about.

THE THINKING PROCESS:

Thinking creates thoughts,

Thoughts create words,

Words create beliefs,

Beliefs create actions,

Actions create habits,

Habits create character,

Character creates service,

Service creates a LIFE.

Thinking is the hardest work there is. That's why so few do it.

I am responsible for *my* life.

I love myself to fully live.

I can only love others IF I love myself.

I forgive myself and everyone else to fully live.

I become what I think about.         I attract what I think about.

I determine what I want to be, do and have and focus on it.

I can have anything I want IF I help enough other people get what they want – this is service.

Life flies by – the older I get the faster it goes.

I live my life in the breaths and moments, not in the days, weeks or years.

The pursuit of happiness and success is a lifelong continuous process. I'll enjoy the pursuit.

Every person is important – all people are equal with different skill sets.

People will forget what I said, forget what I did, BUT always remember *how* I made them *feel.*

Today, at this moment, I am the summation of every thought and decision I have ever made up to this point.

I am very grateful for all that life has taught me and provided for me.

I choose to power my life with love and kindness to fully live.

I choose to *look for good* and it always appears.

I accept the world the way it is and not the way I want it.

My purpose on this earth is to build loving relationships by living a life of: love, joy, peace, patience, kindness, goodness, faithfulness, gentleness and self-control.

My mind is its own place and, in itself, can make heaven of hell or hell of heaven.

I am a human being. My thinking increases my being. My being increases life.

I am not afraid of death – it's only the last step on my path to eternal life.

*Look for Good* and it always appears.

# MY LIFE IS ABUNDANT
**(Compiled since 1981)**

I become what I think about. I attract what I think about.

# LOOK for THINKING   1

> Thinking means to form and have in the mind, especially thoughts, ideas and intentions. It indicates using intellect, reflecting, analyzing and choosing thought priorities and changing thoughts; to reason, conceive, imagine, ponder and envision ideas. It means being cognitive, contemplative, meditative or reflective.

My life is what my thoughts make it.

Thinking creates thoughts - creates words - creates beliefs - creates deeds - creates habits - creates character - creates service - creates a LIFE.

I am master of my thoughts. Thoughts become things.

I think about what I want to be, do and have.

I know there is an unlimited supply of ideas available to me.

I think of possibilities and become creative.

I can change my future and change my thinking by choosing to change my thoughts.

I always have a choice of what to think and how to act.

I am always ready to sit awhile and think. I carve out time to think.

The choices I make, make me.

My future is shaped by my current thinking.

What I think is my reality. My mindset creates my reality.

Thinking is the hardest work there is. That's why so few think!

Be still and think, "What do I want?"

I only think about what I do want and never about what I don't want.

*Look for Good* and it always appears.

Cause and effect: my thoughts are the cause and everything I see, experience and touch are the effect.

Every problem has a solution reachable by thinking.

If it has been done by someone else, it *can* be done and I can do it too.

I am the summation of every thought and decision I have made up to this point.

Answers come to me when I have thought about the question long enough.

I cannot solve my problem with the same thinking I used to create the problem.

I really can't teach anyone anything. I can only present the information or experience to an open mind to be learned.

I do the best I can until I know better. When I know better, I do better.

My thoughts are seeds and they will grow into my life. What I focus on, think about and give my time to, I "feed" and it blossoms.

I take control of my life by taking control of my thinking, thoughts and mind.

I follow my own thoughts, path, truth, heart and joy, as I *look for good* everywhere.

Every great accomplishment in the world was once a single idea in the mind of one person.

I am absolutely clear in my mind about what I want in life and continually think, speak and act on it.

My thoughts are like a magnet and will attract my "want" and draw it to me.

Human ingenuity is limitless. I am the creator of my destiny.

I become what I think about. I attract what I think about.

---

I become what I think about.     I attract what I think about.

My mind is its own place and, in itself, can make heaven of hell or hell of heaven.

*Look for Good* and it always appears.

# LOOK for LOVE    2

> **Love is a feeling you get when you always *Look for Good* in people, places, situations and things.**
> **It is where there are deep, strong, positive feelings of affection and fondness; to be enthusiastic and really liking; to be attracted to or adoring a person, thing or activity. Your heart tells you that you really care.**

I am love and always *look for good* in people, places, situations and things.

Love is only love when I give it away.

Love creates harmony and builds loving relationships.

I love myself and have great respect for who I am.

I love and appreciate the miracle of my body and mind just the way I am.

I love people exactly as they are without judgement or expectations – live and let live.

Life is short, there is only time for loving.

I love and approve of myself and I am worthy of the very best in life.

As I love and respect myself, others will love and respect me.

When I praise someone, I am loving them.

Love and kindness power my life.

I am in love with my life. I don't just feel love; I am love.

The more love I give and use, the more I have to give and use; I can only give what I possess.

I become what I think about.     I attract what I think about.

Love is the fuel that burns my divine sparks.

What I love makes me feel fully alive.

Love is my truest "now" moment. Love is the foundation of every "now" moment.

The love of liberty is the love of others; the love of power is love of oneself.

I love everyone I can; I love everything I can. The love I give out returns to me many times over.

LOVE is Service – is Joy – is Now – is Purpose – is LIFE.

Love heals all. The path to love is forgiveness.

Love has no limits and no boundaries.

Almost everything I see is either an act of love or a call for love.

When I give love to those I meet, it returns to me in abundance.

*Look for Good* and it always appears.

# LOOK for KINDNESS 3

> **Kindness is being friendly, thoughtful, generous, considerate, caring, charitable, giving and helpful to others.**

Kindness and love power my life.

Kindness, given to others, returns multiplied.

Be kind, we need one another. Act like it.

Be kind, everyone has a tough life.

Kindness has no season and is always appreciated.

Three things are important in life: kindness, kindness, kindness.

Kind words can be short and easy to speak but their echoes are truly endless.

A smile is the light in the window of the soul indicating that a kind heart is at home.

Always remember the power of kindness.

*Kindness* creates *kindness* creates *kindness*....

I would rather be a small kind, loving nobody than an evil somebody.

When I truly live in the current moment with kindness, gratitude and mindfulness, my everyday experiences can feel like paradise.

People really welcome a kind word of appreciation, encouragement or a pat on the back. It is an assurance that they are not alone.

When I speak with kindness and truth, I will never have to whisper or apologize.

Smiles always reach the hard to reach places.

I become what I think about.    I attract what I think about.

It is impossible to give a hug without getting one back.

A great kindness to others is when I listen to their smallest ideas or thoughts.

I am worthy of all the kindness and compassion life has to offer.

I show more kindness than seems needed because it is needed more than I know.

*Look for Good* and it always appears.

# LOOK for GRATITUDE 4

> Gratitude means THANK YOU. Gratitude is being and acting grateful, thankful, and appreciative; living in a spirit of joyful appreciation and a grateful heart. It is an affirmation of goodness and encourages more kindness, generosity and gratitude. It produces a feeling of abundance – there is enough for all.

I am grateful – full of gratitude. I am full. I have enough. I have all I need.

All I have in this world is a gift. I am truly grateful for my many gifts.

I begin every day with gratitude and joy. Then I begin my daily quest to *look for good.*

I am grateful for the many lessons I have experienced which allow me to grow and move forward.

Gratitude is only experienced in the moments I open my heart to life, to say "thank you," and really mean it.

Gratitude allows me to be fully present in the present moment – here and now.

Being grateful to others makes me happy.

I choose to remember my gratitude for this earth and all the life it provides.

I have an "attitude of gratitude" – I feel it in my heart and express it – always increasing my "thank you" count.

Gratitude is one course from which I never graduate.

I am grateful for what I need and for my survival.

I become what I think about.        I attract what I think about.

I am grateful for life and health.

I am grateful for people and love.

I am grateful for peace and comfort.

I am grateful for purpose and meaning.

I don't have to almost die to be grateful for this precious day of life – here and now.

I am grateful for the troubled "rocky road" that brought me to the joy and enlightenment of here and now.

Constant gratitude transforms my life for the very best.

The more gratitude I express today for what I have, the more I will have to be grateful for and the fewer regrets I will have tomorrow.

Every gift (birthday, Christmas, food, clothing, shelter, water, air, sunshine, earth, etc.) has a giver and a receiver. As a receiver I am always grateful and thankful.

To people in my life, I say "thank you for being." Your being increases life.

Gratitude is an attitude that can consciously be chosen. It's a choice.

Being grateful and looking for good will always place me in the sunshine of life.

The more grateful I am, the more abundance and fullness of life I sense.

Remember to remember: nothing is guaranteed. Nothing should be taken for granted. I am very grateful for all I have.

*Look for Good* and it always appears.

 for PEACE

> Peace is a state of or an experience of tranquility, calm, quiet, silence or serenity. It is freedom from disturbances, conflict, agitation or commotion.

When I quiet my mind, I find peace.

When I am at peace, I release all anger, resentment, hatred, guilt, fear, regret and envy.

I would rather be peaceful than right.

There is great peace in being at home, my refuge, with those I love the most and with those who love me unconditionally.

I choose not to attend every argument I'm invited to.

Conflict can't survive without my participation.

Peace can only be kept by understanding and compassion, not by force.

Sometimes ignoring things over which I have no control is a great path to peace.

I often find peace by taking a short walk, finding nature and green space, focusing on my breathing or thinking of pleasant places where I find peace.

I find peace and calm when I *look for good* no matter where I am or who I am with.

I make a home within my heart and enjoy being at home with myself. Being alone is not being lonely.

Sometimes I wear headphones to block out sounds that distract my mind.

Photos of the joys of my life keep me grounded and peaceful.

I become what I think about.        I attract what I think about.

I avoid the word "but" because after but comes the *truth*. (i.e., you're smart but…). Use "and" instead.

No matter what happens today, I'll remain calm, serene and relaxed.

Peace is encouraged by stopping and taking ten slow deep breaths.

I find peace in my happy places: favorite meal, dessert, book, music, arts, nature or faith.

Life happens! It is what it is. I let it be. I let it go and go with the flow, peacefully.

I take pleasure and find peace in my own solitude.

*Look for Good* and it always appears.

# L👀K for WELL-BEING 6

> **Well-being is a state of being and feeling joyful, prosperous, comfortable and satisfied.**

I am a blessing to others. I am extending peace, well-being and prosperity to all.

Our deepest craving is to be recognized and appreciated. Always use the Golden Rule.

I am meant to be different from others, to be ME, to be unique.

There is an abundant supply of what's desired for all who really want it.

Each day I remind myself that all is well in my world and I am able to have all my needs met for my body, mind and spirit.

When I can't stand to be alone, it means I don't value my lifelong companion – myself.

My well-being and that of others are totally intertwined and I act accordingly.

I know that what's really important to me is the peace, well-being and prosperity of the people in my life.

There is an unlimited supply of abundance available to me. Life is meant to be abundant.

I always maintain a respect for others and I cultivate their well-being as I cultivate my own.

I am confident that the universe is friendly and life is on my side.

My life is a gift – to me and others. I'll care for it so that it can be fully appreciated by many for a long time.

I will make the *rest* of my life the *best* of my life.

I become what I think about.  I attract what I think about.

# LOOK for PROSPERITY & SUCCESS   7

> Prosperity is a state of being successful, thriving, healthy or with vigorous growth; being strong and flourishing; having steady good fortune and financial security.
> Success is the act of reaching a favorable or desired outcome; attaining or reaching a preferred goal or desire. It is achieving something desired, planned or attempted.

Prosperity and success are never a specific amount of money. They are a state of mind, having the freedom and abundance to do what you want when you want.

Success and excuses have nothing in common. Those who achieve success never rely on excuses and those who rely on excuses never achieve success.

I have enough. I want others to have enough. There is an abundance for everyone, enough for everyone.

Success is 10% of what happens to me (stimulus) and 90% of how I choose to react (response).

The success and high spots in my life have always been connected to supporting and encouraging others.

Success has little to do with what I accomplish, it's all about how I have helped others through service.

I can have anything I want in life IF I help enough other people get what they want—this is service.

Success is the byproduct of service.

Success is the result of a great attitude. A great attitude is not the result of success.

*Look for Good* and it always appears.

Success is often achieved by delaying what I want most instead of settling for less now.

To build a business, I must build up my people and then the people will build the business.

The best way to achieve anything is to expect to achieve it.

Success often happens by hanging on one minute longer.

Some of the world's greatest accomplishments were completed by people who didn't know they were impossible.

Compliments are gifts of prosperity, receive them gratefully.

Success occurs when I have a main purpose or definite goal that I am focused on.

If I love what I do, I will never work a day in my life.

I can never know too many people to be successful. People who like me will want to help me.

My external world of things will exactly correspond to my internal world of thinking and preparation.

Success is best achieved when I'm clear about the goal and flexible with how to get there.

I receive $ _____ each year. (My target annual income from all sources.)

One way to guarantee failure is to quit. One way to guarantee success is to never quit.

I always applaud the success of others. There is a limitless amount of abundance for all of us.

A strong measure of my true life success is how my children describe me to their friends.

I have total control over my attitude and willingness to work hard – two traits that lead to success.

Success principles work. It's people who won't work the success principles who fail.

I become what I think about.       I attract what I think about.

> Forgiveness is the state of forgetting, giving up or releasing resentment, anger or an obligation. It is to absolve or pardon another person; a conscious, deliberate decision to release feelings of resentment or vengeance toward a person; the erasing of an emotional debt.

Forgiveness is the path to love. Love heals all.

Forgiveness of myself and others is a gift to myself and releases me from the past.

Strong people choose forgiveness. Weak people choose revenge.

I am worthy of all kindness, compassion and forgiveness life has to offer.

I am mentally healthy and mature to the degree that I can forgive people who may have hurt me.

A successful, happy relationship is made up of two good forgivers.

Forgiveness is the only way to dissolve the resentment connection with another person and move on to freedom and serenity.

Forgiveness gives me a fresh start, a clean slate, and presents a wonderful new day to fully live.

I forgive and live and let live.

Forgiveness allows me to live in the now and look forward to my future.

I forgive all people for being imperfect and human. Now, we should all try to live the best life that we can.

*Look for Good* and it always appears.

> Compassion is the ability to sympathize, to accept others, to create an understanding or awareness of others' distress and the desire to help or relieve the distress – having pity – to open your heart. It means you are concerned with human welfare and indicates desire to be charitable and merciful due to recognizing suffering, or acting to alleviate the suffering of others.

Follow the Golden Rule: Do unto others as you would have them do unto you.

I treat myself with the same compassion I would extend to my child, spouse or parent.

Great solutions come from recognizing our common humanity and showing compassion.

True compassion comes to me when I realize how little I understand about life and the world around me.

When I can see the situation through the eyes of another person, my perspective will reveal unseen possibilities.

I hear and listen with the intent to understand – not just to reply.

Few are those who truly see with their own eyes and feel with their own hearts.

I am in control of building or dissolving the barriers between my heart and others' hearts. I keep an open heart.

When I make a mistake, I take responsibility and I practice self-compassion.

I am a smart person who uses simple language to communicate.

I am worthy of all the compassion and kindness life has to offer.

I become what I think about.        I attract what I think about.

When I shine the compassion of my human light on others, I change, transform and remake their lives, guiding their path.

Minds are changed through kindness, compassion and understanding, not arguments.

Compassion and criticism should always leave people feeling that they have been respected and helped.

Compassion helps me accept others, whose ways may be different from mine, with gentleness and understanding.

Compassion washes away my anger, distress or resentment and replaces it with love.

*Look for Good* and it always appears.

 for HAPPINESS 10

> **Happiness is a state of well-being and contentment, filled with pleasure or satisfaction and marked by good fellowship, gladness and joy. It is being very pleased and cheerful.**

Happiness is not an end in itself. It is a byproduct of goals and service to others.

Happiness is having goals and progressively fulfilling those goals.

Happiness is about *doing* things – creating, developing and working toward worthwhile goals – not just *having* things.

Happiness is service and meaningful purpose – helping other people.

Happiness requires that I appreciate what I already have.

Happiness is here and now – life in this precious, wonderful present moment.

Happiness involves loving relationships.

Happiness is living in alignment with my values and being myself at all times.

Happiness is in people and experiences – not things.

Happiness is keeping life simple and quiet – being patient, calm, serene and relaxed.

Happiness is being content, whatever the circumstances.

Happiness is acting from a place of service and not ego.

Happiness expectations should be real and match reality.

Happiness eliminates conflict. Conflict cannot survive without my participation.

Happiness is smiling and *choosing* to be happy – it's a choice!

I become what I think about.     I attract what I think about.

Happiness is spending my time doing things I find meaningful and fulfilling.

A happy person never talks bad about other people.

I am always happy to see the ones I love and I let them know it.

I would rather be happy than right.

Of all the things I wear, my expression is the most important. I greet people with a smile.

There is no makeup that creates beauty like happiness.

Happiness is usually delaying what I want most, instead of settling for less now.

One minute of anger is 60 seconds without happiness.

*Look for Good* and it always appears.

 for ATTITUDE 11

> Attitude is what we think about ourselves and our lives. It is the feelings or emotions toward a fact or belief. It is a state of mind (negative, neutral, positive) that affects a person's thoughts and behavior – their mental outlook, feeling or sentiment.

My attitude is what I think about myself and my life.

A poor attitude is everyone's "disability." My attitude has the ability to EN-able me or DIS-able me.

The last of all human freedoms is to choose my attitude in any given set of circumstances, for me to choose my own outlook on myself and on my life.

Life is what it is. I am where I am. Where do I choose to go? That's the question!

A great attitude is a choice – something nobody and no circumstance can take from me.

By altering my attitude, I can alter my life.

It's my attitude that determines my outcome.

I know that in the middle of obstacles and challenges lies opportunity.

I have no limits on my life except those I impose upon myself.

When I am tired, I will rest – not quit.

Mistakes will always happen. Mistakes are opportunities to learn and grow.

Mistakes bring feedback. Grab the feedback and keep on moving forward.

I need to focus on the solutions, not the problems.

I become what I think about.     I attract what I think about.

My attitude toward others determines their attitude toward me.

A great attitude is not the result of success. Success is a result of a great attitude.

I radiate the attitude of well-being and confidence, the attitude of a person with a plan and goals.

A great attitude turns on the lights in my world.

When I catch on fire with enthusiasm, people will come for miles to watch me burn.

Whatever my attitude, people will reflect it back to me.

I have only one life, whether I spend it laughing or weeping – it's my choice.

I want to live, not watch other people live. Attitude is everything.

My attitude is the "glasses" through which I see my world.

Everyone likes to be with an optimist.

I always strive to do better, be better and make the world a better place.

Tough times never last, tough people do.

I need very little in life and most material things, after food, clothing and shelter, really do not matter and are temporary.

I possess or I can acquire all the qualities, knowledge or skills I need to be happy and successful.

Put people first, things second.

I ask you, "Attitudes are contagious, is yours worth catching?"

*Look for Good* and it always appears.

# LOOK for TODAY   12

> Today indicates the present, current times; on or for this day. It is the 24 hours between 12 am and 12 am. It is right now, the present day, time or age. It means to live in the moment, here and now; to be mindful and aware of the very present.

Today is a precious, wonderful day to be alive.

Thank God for Today. (TGFT)

With no plan for today, I am lost before I start.

Time is the most valuable thing a person can spend.

Today I choose my state of mind just as I choose my behaviors and my path in life. So today, I choose something great for myself.

Today I think and act positive. I think about and act on what I want.

Today is all I am guaranteed, I must take action today. Life is now and here.

What I do today is important for I am giving up a day of my life to do it.

Today is for today – I live here, now in the breaths and moments of today.

If not now (today), when? If not here, where?

With today comes new strength, new thoughts and new possibilities.

I begin doing what I want to do now, here. I am not living in an eternity, I live here, now. Do it now!

Every moment I am alive and breathing is a precious one. I choose to use it wisely.

The crisis of today is the lesson for tomorrow.

I become what I think about.     I attract what I think about.

Lack of thinking and goals are the problems, not lack of time. We all have 24 hours per day.

The best thing about the future is that it only comes one day at a time.

Yesterday is history and tomorrow is a mystery. Today is a gift: I unwrap it gratefully with excited, joyful anticipation.

Today wherever I am, I will be all there – here and now.

Today, wherever I go, I go with all my heart.

Today is the best day of my life. It is the only day I have.

Today, when I truly live in the current moment with kindness, gratitude and mindfulness, my everyday experiences can feel like paradise.

Whatever my goals, I will take some action toward them today.

Today is a new day. I am a new me. There are new experiences and new opportunities to create.

Today holds the sum of all my past choices and experiences as well as all my future potential.

I own today. It is mine.

Today is always a great day for learning; I *look for good*.

Tomorrow belongs to the people who prepare for it today.

Family photos remind me of what's important in my life and why.

My best days only happen TODAY.

*Look for Good* and it always appears.

# LOOK for COURAGE 13

> **Courage is to be brave, having mental and moral strength to persevere and withstand danger, fear or difficulty; to meet stress, challenges and difficulties head on. It is having stamina of mind and body to hold one's own firmness of mind and will when opposed or threatened. Courage is a firm determination to achieve one's desires; having stubborn persistence, fortitude, spirit; a quality of mind enabling a person to face danger with bravery.**

Courage is not the absence of fear, it is the awareness of fear and knowing something else is more important.

I can always do more than I think I can.

Courage doesn't always roar. Sometimes it is a quiet voice that says tomorrow is a new day.

It takes courage to listen to and act upon the still quiet little voice in my head.

"I'm sorry" and "thank you" are powerful words that strong, courageous people use.

It takes courage to admit that I am really in charge of my own life and my destiny.

All people are afraid in a battle or conflict. A coward lets fear overwhelm duty. Duty is the essence of maturity.

I welcome adversity and obstacles for they will introduce me to myself.

I have the courage to do the thing I fear and the power will come for me to succeed.

I am always ready to give up the good for the great.

I become what I think about.     I attract what I think about.

Heroism often consists of hanging on one minute longer.

When I climb the "mountain," I can see the "view."

There can be no courage unless you are scared and anxious.

I have the power to improve myself and the power to make it happen.

Many know the way to the goal. Few actually walk it. It takes courage.

Anticipated fear of rejection and failure is worse than the actual rejection or failure.

Fear is a feeling. My thoughts can guide me through it and past it to calmness.

The best <u>o</u>ffense against fear is information and preparation.

The best <u>d</u>efense against fear is information and persistence.

Courage is not the absence of fear, it is the mastery of it.

I make progress when I move from my present place and take a risk.

I have courage to take risks – to love, to learn, to grow, to feel, to be flexible and to fully live.

*Look for Good* and it always appears.

# for CHARACTER 14

> Character is the attributes or features that make up and distinguish a person's presence, reputation or image. It is how they present to others. Character is a person's moral excellence, firmness or soundness of being. It reflects their noble traits and outstanding qualities and the essential nature of the person; possessing grand or impressive ideals or morals arising from superiority of mind or actions; moral or ethical strengths; a person's nature or personality.

I say what I mean and mean what I say – speaking with kindness and compassion.

Don't ask for an easier life, ask to be a stronger person.

The true measure of any person is how they treat someone who can do them absolutely no good.

I am very fortunate when I have someone or something that makes saying goodbye very hard.

As I grow older, I find that the most beautiful qualities of a person are never physical.

I welcome the bad news that I am not going to fit in with everyone. The great ones never do.

The most honest "I love you," comes from my parents. After that, I look at actions, not words!

My children won't remember the long lectures I gave them, but they will remember my character, who I am and my actions.

I must perform in a manner consistent with the way I see myself.

The greatest way to live with honor is to live in alignment with my values and always be myself.

I become what I think about.   I attract what I think about.

I must BE before I can DO; and DO before I can HAVE.

The good habits I formed in my youth have made all the difference in my life.

Character does not consist in possessing honors, but in deserving them.

A measure of a person is how they respond to an abundance of power, money or alcohol.

Great amounts of power, money or alcohol do not change me; they only reveal me.

I have to do my own growing regardless of how tall my parents or grandparents were.

No person is great, if they think they are.

Leadership is the practical application of character.

Life is not about *finding* myself, it's about *creating* myself.

It matters not what I am born, it's about who I choose to be.

My good habits are hard to form but easy to live with; bad habits are easy to form but hard to live with.

It was character that got me out of bed, commitment that created action and discipline that followed through.

My character and integrity will determine my future. Therefore, I carry them with me at all times.

I can teach a better lesson with my life than with my words.

I choose what is true, right and noble over what is fast, easy or fun.

Always tell the truth. Honesty is really the best policy with myself and with others.

I only promise what I can deliver.

My character is demonstrated to others by my words, decisions, priorities and actions.

*Look for Good* and it always appears.

# LOOK for SERVICE 15

> Service is the act of serving; to help or benefit other people through actions and behaviors; contributing to the welfare of others by improving and assisting their good fortune. It is a kindly act or favor, good turn or kindness.

Service is the "rent" I pay for being here. It is the purpose of life and not a part-time job.

When I'm doing what I love, I serve others with a glad heart.

I work hard and make some mistakes. Yet I am far ahead of someone who does not try.

Service is all about how I have helped others, not about what I've gained for myself.

The best way to find myself is to lose myself in the service of others.

I act from a place of service, not ego.

My relationships will mirror my attitude and my personality.

Whatever I truly think, value and believe is always expressed by my actions.

Serving others is the most loving act I can do.

My rewards in life will always be in direct proportion to the value of my service to others.

To increase the size of my rewards, I must increase the quality and quantity of my service to others.

I know there is always a better way to do anything, waiting to be created.

I can have anything I want in life IF I first help enough other people get what they want—this is service.

    I become what I think about.        I attract what I think about.

Greatness is not standing above others, it is standing equal with them and helping them to be the best they can be.

Every person, however small or weak, has something to offer to the good of the world.

Many candles can be lit from my candle, without diminishing my light.

My greatest gift is the gift of time. There is no greater honor or tribute I can bestow to others than to give of my time and take time from my life to serve others and support others in troubled times.

*Look for Good* and it always appears.

# LOOK for JOY    16

> **Joy is a feeling, emotion or condition evoked and marked by well-being, success, good fortune. It's being in a state of delight, gaiety or bliss, having great pleasure; to be songful, laughing and dancing. The feeling of extreme gratification aroused by something good or desired.**

I am the only person in control of my joy. It is in me alone – in me and through me only.

I carry my joy with me or I find it nowhere, not in someplace or some person.

I live life in a spirit of joyful expectation.

Our greatest craving is to be recognized and appreciated. Always use the Golden Rule.

Joy is the feeling of grinning inside.

I smile at every situation, obstacle or challenge. I see each one as an opportunity to grow, learn and improve my strength and abilities.

My one positive thought, word, smile or action can change another's life and bring joy – a miracle.

Shared joy is a lighted candle.

Joy is the reward of giving joy to others.

I can inspire many people. Many people can inspire hundreds. Hundreds can inspire thousands. I CAN make a difference in this world.

My spirit heals with joy.

I will follow my joy – that which touches my heart.

I become what I think about.      I attract what I think about.

> Goodness is the quality of being good: favorable, bountiful, advantageous, agreeable, pleasant, solid, true, honorable, virtuous, right, commendable, kind; having high worth, generous, morally sound, being righteous and upright; living a meaningful and ethical life.

When I *look for good* in people and in life, more of it always appears.

I determine what I want to be, do and have and look for it.

I focus on what I DO want and I never think about what I DON'T want!

Crises tend to bring out the goodness in people, the best in people.

At times of crisis, I look for the kindness and generosity of the helpers.

I will always find and have goodness because there's enough for everyone – life is meant to be abundant.

There is great benefit in repeating a good thing.

Where I send my heart my whole being will quickly follow.

When someone does something good, applaud. Then two people will be happy.

Looking for good will always place me on the bright side of life.

I can give away and still always possess: love, smiles, gratitude, friendship, my word.

I make a living by what I get. I make a life by what I give.

Those who do good, do well.

*Look for Good* and it always appears.

I *look for good* and expect it to come every day, because what I expect usually happens; choose to *look for good* and it appears.

Whatever I believe, expect and look for with confidence, will be found.

All people have a need to be seen, heard and appreciated. We are all fragile to some extent.

When I *look for good* in others, I find the best in myself.

*Look for good* means I am grateful for what *is* good and right and for what I *do* have.

Simply put, I want to live my life actively and mindfully, looking for and doing "good" things.

My generosity makes me feel good and makes my life positive.

I take the path of goodness – for goodness' sake!

Because I exist and I think for myself, I can create and bring great "good" to my world – love, kindness, gratitude, peace, well-being, prosperity, trust, education and abundance.

I become what I think about.     I attract what I think about.

# LOOK for HOPE 18

> Hope means to cherish a desire, outcome or result with great anticipation; to desire with expectation of obtaining or to expect with great confidence – having trustful expectation.

I can purposely choose thoughts of hope over fear.

It may be dark outside now, and the sun will shine in the morning.

I know that things always work out for the best.

To achieve my dreams, I must *be* the person I wish to become.

Life is what it is. I am where I am. Where am I going? I make my own choices.

We always have a choice, even if it is to do nothing. There is always a solution – even if we do not like it.

A society grows great when old people plant trees whose shade they know they will never sit in.

I welcome growing old. It is a privilege denied to many.

I am a rainbow in someone else's cloud. I am a beacon of light to those seeking a ray of hope.

Every person I know today was once a stranger to me.

Every person I meet today knows something I do not.

The smallest action is worth more than the grandest intention.

Which kind of person do I want to be: giver or taker; lover or hater; creator or critic? It's up to me. I choose.

No matter what my history, no matter my story, no matter my circumstance, I can change my future by changing my thoughts.

*Look for Good* and it always appears.

No condition is permanent. Whether good or bad, "this too shall pass."

I am always better when I am with those I love.

If it works for me, I keep working it.

When I open my heart to the world and allow life to enter, all is well.

Life Happens! Life doesn't always go the way I planned. With time, energy, guidance and support, I can create new paths and rebuild hope.

We add value to life when we value others, make ourselves more valuable, and know and relate to what others value.

Whatever I believe strongly, becomes my reality.

I see an obstacle as an opportunity – a blessing in disguise.

When in doubt, always assume the best of others.

With each moment and breath there is an opportunity to change for the better.

There is always a better way to do anything. There is always more to learn.

The best thing about the future is that it only comes one day at a time.

Every day above ground is a great day – looking at the petals and not the roots.

I am blessed with a wonderful group of people – supportive family and friends.

I need to be a source of hope and positivity for all those around me.

Spring reminds me that there is beauty and growth after the troubled gray skies.

I become what I think about.        I attract what I think about.

for PURPOSE & GOALS 19

> Purpose, meaning goals, is an end to be obtained or attained. It is an action in course of execution, an intention of direction or an aim/goal to oneself. Purpose is what one intends to achieve – the aim, goal, intent or target.

I want to live my life on "purpose."

I can make the world a better place.

I am here on earth to fulfill some purpose that only I can offer to the world. I am an amazingly rare, totally non-replicable individual with talents and gifts that the world anxiously needs. The more that I experience the truth of my uniqueness and beauty, the more I will feel gratitude for my particular gifts and the more I will be able to deliver those gifts.

The universe is friendly, I know life is on my side. I must participate.

It's good to have an end to a journey; but it's the journey that matters, in the end.

I always want to be a blessing to others, extending peace, well-being and prosperity.

My life purpose is to build loving relationships.

I welcome life's lessons to help me grow and become my very best.

As long as I'm alive there will be lessons to be learned. I am a perpetual student.

I am a beacon of love, kindness and gratitude. I promote peace, well-being and prosperity through every thought, word and action.

To get ahead, think of a new way to do an old something or think of a new something to do.

*Look for Good* and it always appears.

Anything worth doing is worth doing *poorly*, until I can do it well.

Opportunity is missed by most people because it is dressed in overalls and looks like work.

Achievement is definitely preceded by hard work focused on a specific purpose or goal.

To have what I don't have, I must do what I don't do.

My purpose includes participating fully in life. The only difference between a grave and a rut is the depth.

Life is about relationships with people, places and things. My goal is to always build loving relationships.

As I look forward, I must constantly think, "What's the most important use of my time, right now?"

I am never alone. I have a sense of wonder, a sense of something greater than myself.

I am a part of something bigger and better than myself.

I have a sense of urgency. I must take action now toward my goals.

When challenges and crises confront me, I *look for good* – the lessons and what the moment is teaching me.

# for PATIENCE 20

> Patience indicates waiting with quiet calm and peace; holding oneself back from hurry or effort. It means bearing pains, trials and time with calm resolve. Patience is the capacity of enduring hardship or inconvenience without complaint and being very tolerant.

I am patient, calm, serene and relaxed.

Time is always well invested when it connects two people and makes better friends.

Remember to keep life simple, quiet and peaceful.

To keep your patience is to be in control and win the battle.

I may be a slow walker. I would rather always move carefully forward than ever slide backward.

Patience and tolerance help me peacefully coexist with others.

Life is not always waiting for the storm to pass; sometimes it's about learning to work in the rain.

Sometimes I should pause in my pursuit of happiness and just be happy.

Patience is a tough road to stay on but the surest road to happiness and success.

Appreciating nature and green spaces helps anchor me to the present – here, now.

Patience is a response I can cultivate, giving me the time to think and choose my response carefully.

*Look for Good* and it always appears.

# LOOK for HUMILITY 21

Humility is the act of being humble or unpretentious, modest and in a spirit of submission; having a lack of vanity or self-importance; being grounded.

Humility is often found in people who have bounced back, but still remember how much the fall hurt.

Every person I meet knows something I do not know.

When I talk I repeat what I know. When I listen, I usually learn something.

I treat all people as though they are equal, only with different skill sets.

Be humble and serve others.

Talent is God-given, be humble. Fame is man-given, be grateful.

My greatest opportunities in life lie in the development of my own talents and abilities.

I remember, honor and thank all my teachers, including people and experiences, for their guidance.

Great thoughts and great ideas, like great deeds, need no fanfare.

Owning less is great. Desiring less is even better.

I am richest when I am content with the least.

Keep life simple. Keep food simple—"eat real food, not too much, mostly plants."

I am unique. The world is waiting for my contributions.

Without my uniqueness, my life would be very boring.

I am the overnight success that only took 40+ years.

I become what I think about.        I attract what I think about.

What would I dare to attempt if I knew I could not fail?

I treat everyone I meet with respect, kindness and courtesy as if they were my child, spouse or parent.

I can learn something from every person I meet, even if it is what not to do.

I know that learning never ends.

I would rather be happy than right.

I never miss a chance to be quiet and listen.

I perform at my best when I help others succeed.

*Look for Good* and it always appears.

# LOOK for SELF-CONTROL 22

> Self-control is a state of exercising restraint over one's own impulses, emotions or desires; self-restraint; it is responding to stimulus with a careful, thoughtful, deliberate, mindful response – not reacting.

I am in control of my life.

I can only control myself, not the chaos and circumstances around me.

I have destroyed my enemy when I have made him my friend.

When I am satisfied and grateful for what I already have, I am rich.

I treat everyone the same because we are all equal, only with different skill sets.

My "luck" happens when preparation meets opportunity. Never quit – persevere!

Opportunity dances with those already on the dance floor.

I control everything that enters my mouth. It will only be healthy and supportive, fueling the needs of my body – all in moderation. Nothing ever accidently fell into my mouth.

Self-control is the bridge between goals and accomplishments. Perseverance is the foundation.

Persistence is self-discipline in action. Never give up, never give up.

Self-discovery is one of the best ways to develop a sincere appreciation for my life.

I can achieve whatever I want in life, if I learn what I need to know in order to achieve it.

I become what I think about.     I attract what I think about.

In every setback or obstacle I will look for the seed of a greater benefit or opportunity.

Whatever I tell myself often enough will be accepted as a fact by my mind and will be my belief, so I strive to always think and act positively and focus on what I want.

Habits are like muscles, the more you use them the stronger they get. Choose and use only the good ones.

Self-control means will-power, self-sacrifice and requires a long-term outlook.

I don't want to compete with everyone else, I just want to be the best ME I can be and always improve.

I control myself because I can be my own worst enemy.

Anything worth doing is worth doing poorly, until I can do it well.

It is not the strongest nor the most intelligent who survive; it is the most responsive to change. I must be flexible.

When I can maintain peace and joy within me, despite the activities around me, I am master of myself.

I decide my highest priorities and say NO to all the other choices.

I can learn from other people's mistakes so that I don't have to make those mistakes, myself.

Only when I'm focused, dedicated and self-disciplined, will I have great accomplishments.

*Look for Good* and it always appears.

# LOOK for
# RESPONSIBILITY 23

> Responsibility is to respond with ability and be held to account; to be trustworthy and be able to answer for one's conduct and obligations. It is to know right from wrong and choose for the better; it is marked by accountability, commitment, authorship, ownership and fulfilling a duty.

I am responsible for who I am, everything I have and for everything I become and achieve.

My responsibility begins with me acknowledging and taking charge of my mind and thoughts.

I play a part in each chapter of my life's story. However large or small my part is, I contribute something.

I need to learn the lessons of life so as not to repeat them.

If it's to be, it's up to me.

If I fail to plan, I am planning to fail.

Responsibility is a major lesson of maturity and adulthood.

If I want to teach others responsibility, I must teach by my example.

I empower others and share with others. They will do the same.

Knowing change is inevitable and constant, I am responsible for finding the opportunities within it and flowing with it.

The time is never perfect. The lights are never all green. I just start. I do the best I can and continually make improvements.

To be at my very best I hold myself responsible to a higher standard than anybody else expects of me.

I become what I think about.    I attract what I think about.

I want to be and do everything that's inside me and reach my full potential.

I have a responsibility to use all my powers for good.

Sometimes being done is better than being perfect.

I have a responsibility to give back, to serve others and make a difference so my life matters.

I apologize and admit a mistake, sooner rather than later.

I am responsible for managing my own morale.

A promise made is a debt unpaid.

*Look for Good* and it always appears.

# LOOK for TRUST — 24

> Trust is an assured alliance on the character, ability, strength or truth of someone or something. It is a dependence on something in the future; to depend upon and be confident in and believe without question.

A trusted leader communicates with clarity, conviction and candor, focused on the facts.

The trust bond between any two people is the foundation of a successful future.

Nothing ruins the truth like stretching it.

I trust my brain, the intelligence and intuition I've been given, to lead and guide me.

I have always trusted my own counsel after seeking advice from many. I know myself.

If I am careless with the truth in small matters, I cannot be trusted in important matters.

I can give away and still possess: my trust, my love, my smile, my gratitude, my friendship.

I need very little to be happy. I have enough.

There is an abundance for everyone.

I keep my life simple, quiet, humble and peaceful.

People make my life, special people make my life special.

I need to accept the world the way it is and not the way I want it.

One of the greatest gifts I can bestow on another is my trust and belief in them.

I become what I think about.        I attract what I think about.

> Laughter is to show emotion with joy and explosive vocal sounds indicating amusement, pleasure or approval. It indicates sounds and appearance of happiness and silliness – being comical, funny, humorous or ludicrous.

Laughter is contagious.

I give myself permission to laugh.

Laughter attracts happiness and repels negativity.

The shortest distance between two people is laughter.

The secret to laughter and humor is surprise.

I always look for something to laugh about and find humor in.

I always mix a little humor in with my serious activities. It's great to be silly at the right moment and connect with others.

I laugh at myself and life. It's all temporary. Will it really matter in five years?

A smile is a very inexpensive way to instantly improve my looks.

Smiles beget smiles. Laughter begets laughter. Hugs beget hugs. It's all very creative and connecting.

I always put my brain in gear before my mouth starts moving.

My mind heals with laughter.

**Two riddles, pass them on.**

Where do you send someone who gets injured in a peek-a-boo accident? To the I.C.U.

Why can't you see elephants hiding in trees? Because they're so good at it.

*Look for Good* and it always appears.

# LOOK for
## MINDFULNESS 26

> Mindfulness is being of full consciousness or awareness and giving your full attention to something. It is being concerned and appreciative of, observant of or watchful of; marked by comprehension and perception. It is maintaining an awareness of thoughts, feelings and environment via a gentle and supporting view.

I have only this moment, this breath, not eternity.

I do what I want now – here. If not now, when? If not here, where?

When conflicts and obstacles arrive, I know for sure "This too shall pass."

Mindfulness creates freedom to choose and then act.

Life Happens! It is what it is. I let it be.

Troubles happen. Troubles are my greatest teachers – life lessons to make me stronger.

One original simple idea pursued, is worth 10,000 great intentions.

God gave me a precious, wonderful brain – I use it.

Just because someone told me something, doesn't make it true.

I "remember to remember" what is important to me and act upon it.

Since my mind can only hold one thought at a time, I will make each thought constructive and positive.

*Look for Good:* I look for the best in people, situations and ideas.

I am constantly alert and looking for new ideas that I can put to use in my life.

I become what I think about.     I attract what I think about.

When I truly live in the current moment with mindfulness, kindness and gratitude, my everyday life experiences can feel like paradise.

My future depends on many things, but mostly on me and my thinking.

I carve out time each day to be very still, be mindful and be fully myself.

I try new things because I am mindful and curious of options and possibilities.

I can use *new eyes* to see things I have only looked at before.

Music helps me live in the moment – here, now – when it touches my heart.

Unnoticed beauty is all around me waiting for me to see it. *Look for good.*

I doubt my doubts and believe my beliefs by feeding my beliefs and starving my doubts.

Think of ideas that are sound and good, not ideas that just sound good.

I am the creator of my destiny.

My mind is its own place and, in itself, can make heaven of hell or hell of heaven.

*Look for Good* and it always appears.

# LOOK for HEALTH    27

> **Health is the condition of being sound in body, mind and spirit, especially freedom from physical disease or pain. It is a strong and active wellness of body, mind and spirit.**

The foundation of my health is built on my loving, approving and accepting of myself, just as I am, right here and right now.

I am healthy and healed in body and mind and weigh #_____. (My target ideal weight)

I eat only nourishing and healthy foods.

My body works best on simple food: "eat real food, not too much, mostly plants."

My health will be reflected by my attitude.

I am living to a healthy # _____ years of age. (The target age of my long, healthy life)

How old would I act if I did not know how old I was?

I create good health by thinking and talking about my wellness and longevity.

I appreciate my body and treat it with loving kindness.

I recognize where I am with my health and am ready to change and grow to improve it.

I do all I can to help my body to be as healthy as possible.

I avoid the three "white poisons": salt, refined sugar and flour.

I consume about 30 grams of fiber a day.

I eat lots of whole grain flour, cereals and breads as well as nuts, seeds, beans, fruit and vegetables.

    I become what I think about.      I attract what I think about.

I moderately exercise 90 to 150 minutes per week.

I visit my dentist every six months and have an annual physical.

I choose thoughts that create a healthy and safe atmosphere within and around me.

By *looking for good*, I can help my health and wellness improve.

My body heals with play.

I welcome growing old. It is a privilege denied to many.

I have nothing without my health.

Joyful mental sunshine will cause the flowers of love, kindness, gratitude, peace, well-being, prosperity and happiness to grow around me. I will be a creator of joyful mental sunshine!

*Look for Good* and it always appears.

# AFFIRMATIONS
## (First person, present tense, positive.)

I am alive here and now – a miracle!

I am love – always looking for good.

I love and respect myself. I am good enough.

I am responsible.

I am worthy of the very best.

I am grateful and thankful.

I am master of my thoughts.

I choose and change my thoughts.

I am patient, calm, serene and relaxed.

I am equal to all people.

I am powered by love and kindness.

I am healthy and healed in mind and body.

I am focused on what I want to be, do and have.

I achieve anything I set my mind to.

I receive $_____ each year. (My target annual income from all sources)

I weigh #_____ today. (My target ideal weight)

I am living to a healthy #_____ years of age. (The target age of my long, healthy life)

I trust the "friendly universe."

I am a beacon of love, kindness and gratitude.

I promote peace, well-being and prosperity through every thought, word and deed.

I become what I think about. I attract what I think about.

> I become what I think about.    I attract what I think about.

# SIMPLE LIFE INSTRUCTIONS

**Find peace and freedom as you live your life analogous to the childhood song,**

## *Row, Row, Row Your Boat*

| | |
|---|---|
| *Row, row, row your boat –* | means YOU participate and work hard in your life's duties and fulfill all of your personal responsibilities. |
| *Gently down the stream –* | means you live your life in a calm, serene, and relaxed attitude; going with the flow of life's control and direction (not against it). |
| *Merrily, merrily, merrily, merrily –* | means you are content, comfortable, and happy. |
| *Life is but a dream –* | means you ride life's current to your destiny and reach your goals of abundance, prosperity, happiness and success. |

*Look for Good* and it always appears.

## About the Author

It's probably unexpected that a career mortician would write a book about happiness and success. After actively working 49 years in the funeral service industry, exposed to death and final dispositions for decades, it may seem surprising that I followed this path. My reality, however, is that the more exposure to death, removals, embalming, funeral arrangements, funeral ceremonies, burials and cremation I experienced, the more interest and excitement I had about life and how and why it works and how my thinking directs my life.

Here's the story:

I was born in 1948 and raised in south St. Louis, Missouri. I grew up in a modest home in a working class neighborhood located near the iconic landmark, Bevo Mill Restaurant, which was built by the beer baron, August A. Busch, Sr., in 1917.

My parents were hardworking plain folks who were active in Christy Memorial Methodist Church. My dad, George Richie (born 1906), was a letter carrier and my mom, Gladys Klein Richie (born 1913), was a homemaker. They each had a strong work ethic which was solidly instilled in my upbringing.

I attended local St. Louis public elementary schools (Long and Buder) and was graduated from Cleveland High School in 1966. While attending Southeast Missouri State University (1966-1969), I took a vocational test which guided me to a career in mortuary science. I was graduated from Worsham College of Mortuary Science, Chicago, IL, in 1970.

After completing the license-required internship at D. W. Newcomer's Sons Funeral Home in Kansas City, MO, I was licensed as a Missouri funeral director and embalmer in 1971. This began a funeral service career in the St. Louis area that included employment at Kriegshauser Mortuaries (1971-1981), Professional Mortuary Services Embalming and Crematory Inc. (founder/president, 1982-1993), Irwin Chapel (1993) and John L. Ziegenhein & Sons (1994-2019). At John L. Ziegenhein & Sons, I eventually became owner/president in 2006 and then sold the funeral home business in 2019. At that time, age 71, I stepped into retirement and now work part-time.

After being fired and unemployed in 1981, I began to wonder why some people succeed and other people don't. Thus began a life-long interest in self-help, self-improvement, self-actualization and helping others do the same. I learned that "attitude is everything," "I become what I think about" and that our thoughts actually create our life. This knowledge inspired me to seek out other resources regarding happiness and success.

The years 1981-2019 included a roller coaster path of troubles and joys. This included two divorces, raising three beautiful daughters and finally meeting the love of my life, my wonderful wife, Linda. I wanted answers to simple questions about life, human relations, luck, security, getting ahead, finding peace, happiness and success. It was during these years that I began collecting and compiling statements that are now published in *LOOK For GOOD*, Secrets of Happiness and Success.

Death has inspired me to think about life, love, kindness, gratitude, peace, well-being, prosperity and time – its value and limits. Death has inspired me to say every day, "Thank you God for the gift of this precious new day of life." Death has inspired me to *look for good* and to love and serve others with gladness. Death, it turns out, is only the last step in my life's path to eternal salvation and is not to be feared at all.

I found that LIFE is SERVICE is JOY is HERE/NOW is PURPOSE is LOVE.

I wanted to share these thoughts, ideas and knowledge with you so that you might benefit from my experiences and research and avoid some of the pain of personal setbacks and obstacles. Perhaps the student is ready and the teacher has appeared.

Roger Richie

*Look for Good* and it always appears.

## BOOKMARK
# Cut out this bookmark & fold on the center line, tape together. Use it to keep your place as you continue reading.

| Choose to *LOOK For GOOD* & it always appears. | Choose to *LOOK For GOOD* & it always appears. |
|---|---|
| I am master of my thoughts. Thoughts become things. | I am master of my thoughts. Thoughts become things. |
| I *think* "love, kindness, gratitude, peace, well-being and prosperity." | I *think* "love, kindness, gratitude, peace, well-being and prosperity." |
| I <u>become</u> what I *think* about and I <u>attract</u> what I *think* about. | I <u>become</u> what I *think* about and I <u>attract</u> what I *think* about. |
| Attitude is what I *think* about myself and my life. Poor attitude is my only disability. | Attitude is what I *think* about myself and my life. Poor attitude is my only disability. |
| My attitude has the ability to EN-able me or DIS-able me. | My attitude has the ability to EN-able me or DIS-able me. |

I become what I think about.      I attract what I think about.

*Look for Good* and it always appears.

www.ingramcontent.com/pod-product-compliance
Lightning Source LLC
Chambersburg PA
CBHW071032080526
44587CB00015B/2590